The Yesterday Man

A play

Hazel Wyld

Samuel French – London
New York – Sydney – Toronto – Hollywood

CHARACTERS

Phil Gould

Dora Gould

Terry Bailey

May Bailey

For Jimmy who held my hand through all the bad days.

THE YESTERDAY MAN

The stage is set in two parts. R is a shabby kitchen-diner of a council house on a busy estate in West London. It is a drab, untidy room. Upstage is a sink, a cooker and various cupboards. Over the sink is a window. DL are two large sagging armchairs. There are two doors on the right hand wall. DR is a door to the street and UR a door to the hall. There is a drop leaf table between the two doors. The only other furniture is a small coffee table to the left of one armchair. There are papers and magazines scattered around the floor and a basket of ironing by the sink

The area L represents the Baileys' home next door. The set consists of an ironing board, a clothes horse and a wooden windsor chair. This remains dark until lit by a spotlight when required

When the CURTAIN rises Phil Gould, dressed in his shirtsleeves, is sitting in his kitchen-diner watching television and drinking a cup of tea. He is around forty-five years of age—a genial character, not too bright but loyal and friendly

There is a ring at the street door and he switches off the television and opens the door

Phil Terry! Oh no!

Terry Bailey stands grinning at him from the doorway. He is a tall attractive man in his middle forties, very much a swinger both in his dress and his general attitude. He is carrying an airline bag and wears dark glasses. His casual jacket is wet as is his hair

Terry Hallo, Phil.
Phil (*blocking Terry's entrance*) Terry! What the ... you can't come in, mate, Dora's only up the off licence, she'll kill me!
Terry Come on now, don't start playing silly buggers. It's pissing down out here, I'm getting soaked! (*He pushes past Phil and walks in, looking round the room with interest*) Blimey! You've still got the same wallpaper!

Phil After twenty years! Don't be daft!

Terry (*putting down his bag*) Only kidding. How are you mate? (*He embraces Phil*)

Phil (*uncomfortably*) It's good to see you, but honestly you can't stop.

Terry (*taking off his jacket and sitting down*) Stop panicking. What's the problem? Haven't you told her yet? I thought you were supposed to do that before I got here!

Phil (*sitting down*) I know I said I would. (*Awkwardly*) When you told me on the phone you were flying over . . . well, I thought I could tell her—after all it's not my fault. I've tried for days—I couldn't seem to find the words. After tea I thought you'd be ringing up any time, that's why I sent her up the off licence, to get some booze. I decided if I got her a bit tiddly . . . I mean . . . blimey Terry! First I've got to tell her I kept in touch with you behind her back, then I've got to tell her you've come back for the wedding and, just for good measure, throw in you've decided she's the right person to break the news to May! I tried. I couldn't just . . . I mean . . . Strewth . . . It's not easy!

Terry Obviously! (*He searches through his jacket for a cigarette*)

Phil It wouldn't be so bad if the wedding wasn't tomorrow.

Terry (*patiently*) It's because the wedding is tomorrow that I'm here, mate. Don't get het up, she'll be all right—once she gets over the shock!

Phil (*unhappily*) Yes, of course. I just didn't expect you to turn up here. (*He stands and runs his fingers through his hair*)

Terry What did you expect me to do? Wait at the airport?

Phil (*vaguely*) I dunno, ring up later like I said, after I'd told Dora, tell us where you were staying, arrange a meet or something.

Terry I don't know where I'm staying yet, I came straight from Heathrow.

Phil Maybe you shouldn't have come at all. Dora's gonna go mad, this will be all my fault.

Terry (*easily*) They might both take it better than you think, May and Dora, I mean, you can never tell with women. Anyway I'm here for my daughter's wedding, no crime in that, is there?

Phil (*doubtfully*) No, of course not, but if you haven't been around for twenty years, well it's bound to cause a stir turning up on the wedding eve, ain't it!

Terry (*confidently*) I know my May, after she's got over the shock, she'll be over the moon.

The Lights fade on the Goulds' kitchen and a spotlight comes up L on May Bailey, standing ironing a bridal veil. She is slim and attractive, and although in her early forties, she looks younger. She is holding a cordless phone and talking whilst continuing to iron with the other hand

May (*on the phone*) Don't ask me! I'm the last one to give advice, it's so long since I had a husband I'm practically a virgin! (*She laughs*) I'm kidding, I'm kidding! I don't know what I'd advise, honestly I don't . . . No, I'm all alone . . . Jack's at the stag night and it's Tracey's hen night. . . . No. I had to go and see to Mum . . . Oh just a cold. . . . Well you wouldn't expect her to admit that! . . . Double pneumonia at least! . . . Oh she'll be there right enough, wild horses wouldn't keep her away! She'll turn up if only to tell me I mismanaged the whole thing! . . . Of course you aren't! . . . Don't be daft! . . . I mean it! Oh . . . right . . . Hang up quick then. . . . See you in church tomorrow.

The Lights fade on the Bailey household and come up on the Goulds' where Phil is peering anxiously out of the window over the sink unit. Terry is sitting in the armchair DS, quite unconcerned and glancing through an evening paper he has found on the floor

Phil (*nervously*) She's a long time!
Terry For God's sake stop poncing about as though you were waiting for a police raid! Aren't you master in your own house?
Phil Not so's you'd notice. (*He turns to face Terry*) How are we going to handle this?
Terry She's your wife, you tell me!
Phil (*going back to gaze out of the window*) My suggestion would be that I go out . . . and you tell her!

Terry laughs

Oh my God! She's coming! Quick, hide!
Terry Don't be a prat.

Dora enters from the street door. She is a cheerful rather blousy woman in her mid forties, and is carrying some cans of beer. She turns in the doorway and kicks off her shoes

Dora (*talking happily*) Bloody hell, what a night, I hope it's not like this tomorrow, they won't be able to get any pictures. I got beer, that all right? (*She turns and sees Terry*) Oh my God no! Please no! (*She clutches her chest dramatically*)

Terry Hallo Dora, still as sexy looking as ever, I see!

Dora What the ... (*She closes her eyes*) Please God, let this be one of them mirages.

Phil (*desperately trying to sound innocent*) I opened the door and there he was.

Dora (*recovering*) Well he can just bugger off back to wherever he's come from. (*She slams the cans down on the table and glares at Terry*) What made him think he was welcome round here.

Terry (*unrepentantly*) Hallo! I am here, in the flesh, I do answer direct questions!

Dora (*leaning menacingly towards Terry*) Do you take direct hints? You're not welcome. Bugger off back where you came from.

Terry Well that's a nice thing to say to an old friend after twenty odd years, I must say!

Dora (*folding her arms*) You're no friend of mine. Does May know you're back?

Terry (*patiently*) I'm not back, Dora, I just popped over the pond for my daughter's wedding, that's all.

Dora Oh that's all! You must be bloody joking! Who told you your daughter was getting married I'd like to know? On second thoughts don't tell me! Let me guess! What do you know about this? (*She turns on Phil*)

Phil (*miserably*) I didn't know he was going to turn up here tonight.

Dora That's not what I asked! Who told him about the wedding?

Phil says nothing

(*Turning back to Terry*) Well, that answers that doesn't it? You'd better start talking and fast. I want to know exactly what is going on, and just remember one thing, your ex-wife is my best friend and always has been. I don't want any lies neither, just the plain facts. Start talking!

Phil (*bravely*) May might be your best friend, Dora, but Terry is mine, we were in the cubs together, we're blood brothers we are, we slashed our fingers and mingled blood.

Dora (*astonished*) When was this?

Phil In the infants.

Dora God give me patience! What are you talking about? He might have been your best friend once but he's been missing for twenty years.

Phil (*defiantly*) Not to me he's not. We've kept in touch, we've always kept in touch.

Dora Kept in touch! What do you mean "kept in touch"? I think you'd better both start explaining yourselves!

The Lights fade on the Goulds' kitchen and come up on the Baileys'. May is now ironing a bridesmaid's dress. A few seconds pass whilst she hums happily to herself. She finishes ironing the dress and puts it on a hanger

May There, that's better. I'll just press the slip and then I think I deserve a drink. (*She takes a long waist petticoat from the clothes horse and puts it over the ironing-board*)

There is a knock at the door

Come in.

Dora enters. She is obviously keyed up to break the news and this should be conveyed by a suggestion of being ill at ease and trying to cover it up

Dora I thought I'd pop round and see how the rehearsal went.

May Fine. Sit down and I'll make us some coffee as soon as I've finished, or would you prefer something stronger?

Dora Yes. (*She looks sympathetically at her*) You look knackered.

May So I am. I know now why the bride's mother cries at the wedding, sheer bloody exhaustion. Go on, take the weight off your feet.

Dora sits and May continues ironing

May Last thing, I promise.

Dora Everything ready now?

May Everything I've got to do ... thank God we're having caterers. If I'd had to do the food as well, I couldn't have coped. I'd be in my grave, I tell you straight!

Dora (*bracing herself*) You've been a good mother to those two kids, bringing them up on your own and everything.

May No more than millions of women have done.

Dora It can't have been easy.

May (*laughing*) Oh I don't know, listening to some of my friends perhaps it was better! I had Lyn on the phone earlier, Bob's off the rails again.

Dora (*doggedly*) Still, I take my hat off to you.

May (*amused*) Well, thank you.

Dora (*trying to sound casual*) How long is it since Terry left?

May Twenty years.

Dora Twenty years! Yes. I suppose it must be . . . Do you . . . ever think of him?

May Terry? Not if I can help it! Not any more . . . Well, sometimes I think of the day I got that telegram, I mean it's not something you're likely to forget, is it? A telegram saying your husband's run off to America with another woman . . . Silly bugger sent it on a greetings telegram, if you remember! Talk about adding insult to injury!

Dora (*hastily*) You must have some happy memories though.

May I did have, but they tend to get wiped out by something like that. Still it's all water under the bridge. Remember the days you, Phil, me and Terry used to go dancing and night clubbing. (*She muses*) Before we had the kids . . . When we were all young and carefree . . . We had some laughs—who'd have thought how it would turn out . . . (*She sighs*) You got the best of the bargain, straight as a die, your Phil.

Dora (*sarcastically*) Oh yes! (*Adding hastily*) I wish he had a bit more go in him, though. Your Terry was always a card, such a Jack the lad. The things he used to get up to! I used to worry in case he was a bad influence on my Phil . . . (*She falters and then brightens*) Still, he was a laugh though.

May (*drily*) Yes? I'm laughing all over my face! Count your blessings reliable old Phil didn't run off with some little scrubber, leaving you to bring up two toddlers on your own. I ask you! What kind of man leaves you and sends you a bloody telegram instead of telling you face to face.

Dora (*carefully*) Don't you ever wonder where he is?

May I know where he is, don't I? America! Well, last I heard he was. Knowing him he's either a millionaire, dead or in the Mafia, no half measures with Terry.

Dora How would you feel if he walked back into your life again?

May (*shuddering*) What are you trying to do, give me nightmares?

Dora I just mean ... well Tracey's wedding day—the timing would be right.

May Leave it out! The timing would be lousy. Can we change the subject? Tonight of all nights I don't want to remember Terry.

Dora (*gamely*) Come off it! This is me you're talking to. I refuse to believe you haven't thought about him a bit lately, I mean with Tracey getting married and all.

May (*sighing*) Yes ... I suppose I have, now and again. Funny thing is he's cropped up in the conversation round here once or twice lately, perhaps he's been on all our minds.

Dora (*carefully*) How do you feel about him—honestly? All these years later.

May I dunno ... I wonder sometimes what he'd think of the kids ... what they'd think of him ... whether he ever thinks of us ... Oh, you know the sort of thing.

Dora Yes. May ... I ... Oh God, this is so hard ...

May What's the matter?

Dora (*getting up and wandering round the room*) You know you're my best friend—always have been. If it doesn't sound soppy, I love you dearly. You and me ... well, we go back a long way ...

May (*stopping ironing*) What is it? Is something wrong?

Dora (*taking a deep breath*) It's Phil.

May (*concerned*) What about Phil?

Dora I swear I didn't know. Please believe I didn't know.

May (*blankly*) Didn't know what?

Dora (*sitting down again*) He ... Phil, that is ... Oh sweet Lord ... He ... (*In a rush*) Well, he and your Terry ... they've been in touch.

May (*stupified*) In touch?

Dora (*hastily*) I didn't know!

May (*slowly*) What do you mean, in touch?

Dora He used to phone him sometimes.

May (*baffled*) Phil used to phone Terry?

Dora No ... Terry used to phone Phil ... at work ... sometimes ... not regularly ... since he left.

May Dear God.

Dora (*near to tears*) I didn't know, Phil never told me, he knew I'd tell you.

May Dear God.

Dora From America ... Just sometimes, now and again, every so often ... Just to ask how things were—you know, you and the kids.

May Dear God.

Dora Don't keep saying that! Can I get you something? A drink?

May (*faintly*) No ... go on.

Dora I'm so sorry, I truly didn't know until tonight.

May (*bewildered*) So why did he decide to tell you tonight?

Dora (*taking a deep breath*) Maybe you should be the one sitting down.

May Bad as that is it?

Dora He's here—Terry I mean.

May (*blankly*) Here? In England?

Dora In the *Red Lion* actually.

May (*dumbfounded*) He's staying in the *Red Lion*?

Dora No ... he's staying with us ... I mean I just asked him—he had nowhere to stay.

Black-out on the Bailey kitchen and the Lights come up on the Goulds' kitchen

The street door opens and Phil walks in followed by Terry

Terry Well, it comes to something when you can't get near the bar in your own local.

Phil Hardly your local, mate, you've been gone twenty years.

Terry (*testily*) I wish you'd stop saying that! All I've heard from you and Dora tonight is (*mimicking*) "You've been gone twenty years".

Phil (*reasonably*) Well, you have.

Terry I know that, don't I? You don't have to keep reminding me, I know I've been gone twenty years. I'll tell you something else too, not a day passed when I didn't think about them—May and the kids—missing them I mean.

Phil (*puzzled*) Why didn't you come back then?

Terry Well, I couldn't could I? I'd burnt my boats. (*Righteously*) Besides I had to think of young Sylvie, didn't I? I was responsible for her.

Phil (*confused*) Sylvie?

Terry The girl I went off with. A bit of a kid that's all she was ... I could hardly abandon her in a strange country now, could I?

Couldn't bring her back either. Rumour had it her old man was looking for me with a shotgun ... unlicenced ... dodgy family ...

Phil Some people might say you'd abandoned a wife and two kids in the first place ... (*Hastily*) Not me! Here! I wonder what's going on next door, I wish I was a fly on the wall!

Terry Dora will handle it ... after all she's May's best mate, if she can't soften her up no-one can ... I think deep down she's got a soft spot for me ... your Dora ... she'll do her bit all right.

Dora enters from the street door DR *and stands with her hands on her hips glaring at the two men*

Dora I thought you were taking him out till later!

Phil The *Red Lion* was packed out, we couldn't get near the bar.

Dora Well take him somewhere else for heaven's sake, May's coming over in a second, I told her he wouldn't be back just yet.

Terry Well that's all right, just let her walk in and get it over with. How did she take it?

Dora (*sarcastically*) Oh, she was thrilled to bits. She wants to speak to you privately, but round here, she doesn't want you going round her house. (*She turns to Phil*) Just get him out of here for ten minutes that's all I ask ... I don't want her walking in and finding him here.

Phil I don't see what difference it makes.

Dora (*shouting*) I didn't ask your opinion, did I? Just get him out of here, all right?

Phil All right ... keep your hair on ... come on, Terry, maybe we can get a quick pint at the *Bell*.

Terry gets up reluctantly and the two men head for the exit DR

Dora (*shouting after them*) And one pint only ... don't take too long, I want you back here in ten minutes I said!

Terry and Phil exit

Dora starts to hurriedly tidy up by shoving papers etc. into any available cupboard. She lays a tray with glasses and a bottle of Scotch. There is a ring on the doorbell. She goes over to the street door and opens it

May enters

Dora Come in, they're not here.

May (*hesitating in the doorway*) I don't want to do this, I don't want to see him. (*She turns to go*)

Dora (*sharply*) You don't want him knocking on your door, do you?

May He wouldn't!

Dora I should think he might, he's hardly come all this way for nothing has he? Do you want him making scenes round your house?

May (*Looking at her balefully and reluctantly moving over to an armchair*) No I do not ... oh God, why me ...? what have I done to deserve this? What right does he think he's got to walk back into our lives after all these years. I'll never forgive your Phil.

Dora (*bringing the tray of drinks to the coffee table*) I know how you feel ...

May No you don't, how can you? I don't know how I feel. I'm in shock.

Dora I wanted to kill my Phil, once I heard the whole story ... but then I stopped and thought ... suppose you'd run off ... would I have kept you informed about Terry and the kids? ... course I would, so really Phil's just done what I'd have done. I can't believe he's kept a secret, mind you, he's never kept a secret from me in his life ...

May (*bitterly*) How'd you know? I mean you didn't know he'd kept this one did you? He might have a whole load of guilty secrets you haven't found out about yet! (*She walks up and down agitatedly*) They're all bastards! You can't trust one of them, they all stick together. Terry left us, me and the kids, he walked away, by my reckoning that means he's not entitled to know anything. I tell you straight, I've only come to meet him to warn him off ... he's not ruining Tracey's wedding day ... pour me a drink for God's sake.

Dora pours her a stiff whisky. May wanders round the room in an agitated fashion clutching the drink in her hand

The street door opens and Phil enters closely followed by Terry

Phil I forgot the ...

May (*icily*) Hallo, Terry.

Dora (*after a slight pause*) Indian.
Phil (*blankly*) What?
Dora You can take me for an Indian ... come on.

Dora moves towards the door where Terry still stands warily looking at May

Phil I thought you wanted us to ...
Dora Bit bloody late now, isn't it?
Phil (*light dawning*) Oh! You mean ... (*He moves to follow Dora then hesitates and looks at Terry*) What about you mate?
Dora Oh, give me strength!
Phil I only thought ... ? Shall we get you a takeaway?
Dora (*dragging him by the arm*) We're not going for a bloody takeaway ... you are buying me a sit-down meal, dummy.

Phil and Dora exit, leaving Terry and May alone

Terry (*making a valiant effort*) Poor old Phil, his feet hardly touched the ground ... Dora still rules him with a rod of iron, I see.
May Hardly ... or you wouldn't be here!
Terry Can I join you in a drink? I feel in need.
May Help yourself.

Terry pours himself a small scotch, hesitates, looks at May and fills the glass to the brim

Terry Bit of a surprise, eh? Me turning up like the proverbial bad penny.
May (*still very calm*) What do you want, Terry?
Terry (*playing for time*) What do you mean, "what do I want".
May I'd have thought it was a simple enough question, what do you want with us after all these years, what are you doing here?
Terry (*jovially*) My word you're a cool customer, May. Is that all you've got to say after twenty years?
May There is a great deal I could say but I am trying to restrain myself, I just want to get this over with.
Terry (*easily*) Don't do that, May! (*He sits down in an armchair and casually drapes his leg over the arm*) Hell, I behaved badly, I deserve a bollocking, I fully expected to get one! Don't you restrain yourself girl ... get it off your chest.

May gapes at him utterly speechless for a second

She rushes DS *in a fury and starts hitting him over the head*

Terry puts his hands up and tries to protect himself

May God almighty. . . . you arrogant pig! You behaved badly! Is that how you see it? . . . you deserted us! . . . all of us . . . me and the kids! . . . abandoned us! You walked out and left us for some little scrubber and then you stroll back in twenty years later and say you behaved badly!

Terry (*grabbing her arms*) Hey, hey! Calm down, you'll do me an inury.

May (*struggling and panting*) I'd like to do you an injury . . . you . . . cowardly creep. You never even told me you were going, you sent me a bloody telegram . . . you buggered off to America with a nineteen year old and sent me a sodding telegram . . . "behaved badly" . . . Why you, you . . . you miserable bastard.

Terry (*shocked*) Well, your language has taken a turn for the worse I must say, May . . . I always thought of you as a lady.

May (*putting her face close to his*) A lady! Well now! Did you? Funny . . . I always thought of you as a human rat . . . beneath contempt, the scum of the earth . . . and the only reason I came round here, was to make it plain that if you've got any thoughts about turning up at my daughter's wedding tomorrow, forget it . . . if this is what it's all about, you're out of your mind . . . you are not going to be there, because if you walk into that church tomorrow, Terry, if you even stand outside you will be dicing with death. I'll take a sharp knife to church with me and I'll stab you in the back as soon as look at you. I'd say in the guts but you don't have any. Crawl back into whatever gutter you came out of . . . we don't want any part of you.

Terry (*wounded*) There's no need for all this May, no need for the verbals! I have a daughter getting married tomorrow, I don't think it's that odd that I should want to be there.

May You don't think it's odd!

She wrenches herself away from his grasp

Well I think it's bloody odd. You have no rights at all any more. Can't you get that into your thick head? . . . you forfeited them all twenty years ago! You have a daughter, have you? . . . Big

deal! All you did was father her and any fool can do that!
Fathering a child is the easy part. It takes about thirty seconds,
well, in your case it did. Being there, that's what counts. She
managed to go to school, get the chicken pox, have her tonsils
and appendix out, and all kinds of other functions without your
presence, what makes you think she needs you now?

Terry (*sadly; shaking his head*) You're bitter, aren't you?

May Bitter? (*She slumps down in the other chair*) Me? No . . . what
have I got to be bitter about? (*Calm again*) You walked out on
us, me and your children, never gave us a second thought. How
were we managing? Could I afford to keep the house going?
Could I manage to keep the children? You didn't care, you just
kept walking . . .

Terry (*hurt*) That's not true, all these years I've kept in touch,
through Phil, I kept a check on how you all were . . .

May Oh pardon me, I forgot, that makes it all right of course . . .
what were you going to do if we were in trouble? Come back?

Terry (*quietly*) I've always cared for you, May.

May Of course you have, that's why you ran off . . . You cared for
me so much you deserted me!

Terry Don't keep saying that! I had my reasons . . . that's all I'm
saying . . . I might have played around but a lot of men do that,
I'm not a monster. My problem was, young Sylvie fell in love
with me . . . took it all seriously . . . I was in a fix . . . to tell you
the honest truth she thought she was pregnant . . . forced my
hand so to speak. Her dad was in with a funny crowd . . . I'd
never have left you but for that.

May (*startled*) You what!

Terry looks confused as she starts to laugh hysterically

You're unbelievable do you know that? Some little maneater
thinks she's pregnant so you desert a wife and two children! (*She
shakes her head*) Good old Terry! Couldn't let her down . . . (*She
gets up and stands over him*)

Terry puts his hands up to cover his head

(*Shaking*) You could let us down, couldn't you . . . Oh don't hide
yourself . . . I'm not going to hit you . . . I wouldn't lower myself.
Just don't think you can walk back in here and it's all over-
looked . . . and don't try to wriggle out of it by blaming her for

what you did. I was a good wife to you ... and you probably
forgot to tell her the rules ... that it was all supposed to be fun.

Terry (*with dignity*) I know you were a good wife. Housewife wise
... one of the best ... all I meant was ...

May (*calming down*) Anyway, I'm not interested in the past ...
that's not why I'm here ... I came to sort things ... to talk to
you ... I just want to know what you're up to now ... to find
out what you wanted ... Why you've gone to all this trouble?
Plan to give the bride away do you? Or are you broke? Is that it?
Spot of blackmail, is it?

Terry (*holding up his hand*) Hold on! Let's take the insults as read
... to be honest ... I came here because I want to see my
daughter married.

Again he holds up his hand as she goes to speak

No hear me out, I don't expect to give her away or anything ...

May Good, 'cos you did that twenty years ago.

Terry (*wincing*) Always did have a cutting tongue, didn't you
May? No, like I said, I don't expect to be welcomed into the
bosom of the family, I just want to see her get married, sit
quietly at the back of the church and watch her. Now that's not
much to ask, is it?

May You're a joke, Terry, you always were ...

Terry Come on now, May ... let's face it, you can't stop me can
you? I mean I'd rather it was with your blessing, that's why I'm
here, I could have just turned up at the church, *fait accompli*, so
to speak, but I thought it only right to sound you out first, I
wanted it to be all right by you. Also if you're so anxious not to
spoil her day don't let's have any more cobblers about stabbing
me on the church steps.

May I said you were a joke and that's what I meant. Do you really
think you can slip into a back pew and nobody will notice?
What about my mum? All my relatives? Our friends? Your own
children wouldn't know you if they saw you in the street.

Terry protests

Oh, they've seen photos of us together; when we were younger,
but that's all! They don't know you! They barely remember you.
But all those other people, they'd recognise you all right. It's no

good Terry, it wouldn't work. Too many people are after your hide for what you did to me. (*More gently*) You can't turn up and want to play father after twenty years, you've left it too late.

Terry I'm sorry you feel like that, May ... because whether you like it or not, I'm going to be there.

May (*getting up*) Well that seems to be the end of this conversation then, doesn't it?

Terry Wait! I didn't mean to say that ... please ... here ... give me a few minutes ... sit down ... calm down ... Want a fag? (*He offers her a cigarette*)

May Oh for God's sake (*She sits down again*)

Terry It's been a long time ... want to know something? I thought about you a lot.

May (*without emotion*) That's nice.

Terry I mean it, if it's any consolation I regretted what I did.

May It's not.

Terry When I first rang Phil, a couple of months after I left, it was you I wanted to know about, not the kids. Oh, I missed them of course, but not as much as I missed you.

May What's this? Tactic number two? There is no excuse you can offer me, Terry, you should have had the guts to tell me ... face to face ... you might have at least have had the decency to say goodbye.

Terry It's the old story, if I'd stopped to say goodbye, I wouldn't have gone.

May What film did that come from?

Terry I don't expect you to understand ... I didn't understand myself ... the truth is I fancied her, but I loved you. I had to go ... to realize it.

May (*getting up again*) Oh for pete's sake I don't want to listen to this cobblers ... you just wanted another woman that's all.

Terry (*eagerly*) Want! That's the word, May ... "wanted" I "wanted" her, and want doesn't last, I found that out too late. I thought maybe ... well, never mind.

May Well, what a bloody shame, my heart bleeds for you. I don't seem to remember you asking to come back.

Terry I knew you wouldn't have me, I know your temper. I thought you'd spit in my eye. Or stab me in me vital parts.

May Too bloody right.

Terry I've thought of you all, every day of my life, especially you.

May It won't work Terry. I don't believe a word. You never even
sent the kids a birthday card or a Christmas present.

Terry To be honest, May, I never remembered when their birthdays were.

May looks at him speechlessly

(*He adds defensively*) Well, how many blokes do you think
would remember their kids' birthdays without the wife to
remind them?

May (*truthfully*) I don't know ... (*Hardening again*) Still, I
suppose you remembered when Christmas was?

Terry I just thought it was better if I stayed out of all your lives, I
mean I did write once, when I got settled, offered you a monthly
allowance, you sent me a rude card with a five letter word on it.

May (*smiling*) Yes, I did, didn't I.

Terry (*earnestly*) I was heartbroken when I got that card.

May Balls.

Terry Yes, that was the word.

May Get to the point will you, I want to get some sleep tonight, if
at all possible.

Terry I used to ring Phil and get all the news. I might not have
been around for the chicken pox and the appendicitis and all but
I knew about them, and the tap dancing silver medal and Jack
getting in the First Eleven at school. I made him promise not to
tell Dora, I knew she'd tell you, I didn't want that.

May My heart bleeds for you, Terry, it really does.

Terry (*helplessly*) I'm not the first man who's run off with another
woman.

May This is pointless conversation. I don't want you there
tomorrow. .... I don't want you to spoil Tracey's day ... you've
buggered up our lives enough.

Terry You can't forgive me can you, May? All this bullshit about
your brothers ... do you honestly think anyone else gives a
damn? ... if they think I'm there with your blessing that'll be
good enough for them. At least be honest with yourself ... it's
you who can't forgive ... I'll tell you what ... tell Tracey I'm
here, let her decide.

May No. (*She goes to walk away*)

Terry (*following her*) I'm not leaving till it's sorted.

May (*walking to the street door and opening it*) It can't be sorted
... I'm not giving you my blessing, if that's what you're hoping
for ... I can't stop you from turning up but don't kid yourself
that if you harass me enough I'll give in ... I'm a harder woman
than the one you left behind. You don't belong in this family
anymore ... you're just a man from yesterday ...

Terry grabs her arm and pulls her towards him

Terry Don't keep walking away from me, May ... I've got to ...

*May suddenly bursts into tears, we realize that she is overwrought in
spite of her trying to control the situation. Within a second or so,
Terry is cuddling her. She initially resists but it is too much effort
and she weeps on his shoulder. He shushes her as you might a child
and then pulls out a hanky*

Terry Here ... blow.

May blows her nose obediently

May Oh God.
Terry There ... better.
May Yes, thanks.

*For a few seconds she doesn't seem to notice Terry still has his arms
round her. When she does she immediately moves away*

God, you haven't changed ... drive me to hysterics then you're
right there with the hanky. You're the only man I ever met who
always has a hanky ... I suppose you spend your life reducing
women to the state where they need one. (*Suddenly curious*)
Where is Sylvie? Does she know you've come here? I suppose
you did marry her ... after the divorce went through?
Terry Yes ... her and a couple of others.
May (*startled*) You've had four wives?
Terry Yeah.
May Good grief, once was enough for me! I never wanted to get
married again. (*She walks over to an armchair and sits down,
completely worn out*)
Terry (*simply*) I know, I was glad about that.
May (*drily*) Don't be, it isn't a compliment.

Terry I never had any more kids. That pregnancy turned out to be a false alarm.

May (*sarcastically*) You do surprise me! (*Without rancour*) Daft bugger . . . I used to wonder about that . . . if you had kids . . . I used to think "Please God, don't let him have more children" . . . silly isn't it? . . . I don't even know why . . . it was as if, by having other children you'd be taking something away from ours . . . God knows what! Are you married now?

Terry Separated . . . I'm getting a divorce.

May I see.

Terry You're my only family, May, you three, that's why . . .

May (*holding her hands*) Please!

Terry (*smiling*) So . . . you never had another man then?

May I never said that . . . I said I hadn't married again. Naturally there have been men . . . I'm not a nun.

Terry You what!

May You heard.

Terry How many men?

May (*shrugging*) I didn't keep a score card.

Terry Charming! I never had you down as a scrubber, May, and that's telling you straight.

May (*amused*) I'm sorry if I've let you down!

Terry I'm shocked to be quite frank.

May Really! Why is that?

Terry (*indignantly*) When I left my children in your care I thought I was leaving them with a good woman, a good example, a woman of morals.

May You sanctimonious creep!

Terry Not at all . . . it's different for women . . . well, women who are mothers . . . mothers should keep themselves pure . . .

May You've got a bloody nerve you . . . you pompous chauvinist, one rule for me and another for you! Is that it?

Terry All right . . . put it another way, I never thought you'd play around.

May Well maybe I needed some reassurance after the way you treated me . . . maybe just maybe . . . I was trying to prove to myself that one man is as good as another, in some respects anyway . . . I'll tell you one thing I did find out . . . in and out of bed you aren't anything special . . . and just in case you think that's sour grapes, you must agree that there's at least three other women in the good old U.S. of A who prove me right! None of them seem to have wanted to hang on to you, have they?

Terry You did!

May Not for long, sweetie . . . not for long!

Terry Hurt pride that's all you suffered from . . . let's be honest, you'd lost interest in me anyway, except as a possession, a husband in inverted commas . . . you'd given up trying.

May That's a lie.

Terry Is it? Is it really, May?

May One question and one only, Terry . . . did you come back to see your daughter married? Or was it a good excuse to get your foot back in the door? I mean now that you've ballsed up your life generally . . . did you think, "Maybe I should have stuck with the first wife . . . let's give her another whirl".

Terry I came to see my daughter married.

May Really. (*She walks upstage to the street door*) I'm going home . . . don't try to stop me and don't follow me . . . do as you please about tomorrow . . . you usually do . . . and if you decide to come I hope my brothers give you the hiding of your life, I hope your children cheer them on, I hope you crawl on broken knee caps on to that plane back to America . . . and for good measure I hope you open the wrong door halfway across the Atlantic and fall out.

May exits through the street door

Terry watches her go, genuinely surprised

Terry (*calling after her*) Have I said something to upset you . . . May? I thought we were beginning to talk, I want us to talk.

Black-out for a few seconds

A spotlight comes up on the Bailey's kitchen which is empty. May enters in a rush, stops in the doorway out of breath and after a short pause she crosses and kicks over the clothes horse. She bursts into tears

The Lights come back up in the Goulds' house. It is the following morning and the day of the wedding. Apart from the fact the bottles and glasses are not visible the room looks as it did the night before

Phil, dressed in his best suit plus buttonhole, is standing looking anxiously at his watch

Phil (*shouting*) Terry? Dora?

Dora enters. She too is all dressed for the wedding and appears out of breath

Dora Shout a bit louder, why don't you?

Phil What did she say?

Dora She's coming over in a minute . . . she seemed a bit surprised . . . said when she left here last night he was dead set on coming to the wedding.

Phil He was a bit quiet when we got in . . . stayed up half the night too . . . I heard him moving about.

Dora He didn't say anything to you? After I went to bed.

Phil No, he didn't say a dickie bird . . . I did ask how it went but he changed the subject.

Dora Well anyway she's coming over.

The internal door opens and Terry enters. He is wearing his coat and carrying his airline bag. He walks to the window and looks out

Phil watches him in silence, obviously concerned

Dora (*watching Terry suspiciously*) I told her you were leaving and wanted a word and she's coming over in a minute.

Terry (*without turning*) Thanks.

Dora I should think so too . . . it was like a madhouse over there . . . it wasn't easy getting her alone for a . . .

Terry (*still without turning*) I appreciate it.

Dora (*shrugging*) Come on, Phil . . . let's get to the church.

Phil (*looking at Terry*) Don't you think it's a bit early to . . .

Dora (*firmly*) No I don't . . . out.

Phil (*touching Terry's shoulder awkwardly*) Best of luck, mate.

Terry clasps his hands and says nothing

See you on the ice.

Phil hesitates and then moves to the door where Dora is waiting impatiently

You know where I am . . . I mean . . . if you need me.

Terry (*still looking out of the window*) Thanks, mate.

Phil reluctantly follows Dora out of the street door

There is a slight pause

May stands in the street doorway. She is wearing a housecoat and was obviously getting dressed ready for the wedding when summoned

May Dora said you were off to the airport!

Terry (*without turning round*) That's right.

May Changed your mind about the guest appearance then, have you?

Terry Looks like it.

May What brought on the change of heart?

Terry It's what you wanted, isn't it?

May Since when has what I wanted had anything to do with your actions?

Terry It seems to matter quite a bit.

May Since when?

Terry (*turning to look at her*) Well, to tell you the truth, May, I don't give a damn about your brothers . . . just you.

May Terry . . . stop it.

Terry It's the truth . . . I've always loved you, why do you think I ran away instead of facing you like a man? I was more frightened of what you'd say when you found out Sylvie was pregnant than I was of running.

May She wasn't pregnant. It was a put up job that you fell for . . . bloody stupid that's what you've always been. So, you're going back because of me . . . not staying to see Tracey married . . . because I don't want you to? Is that the idea? Is that what you're saying?

Terry I know you don't believe it but I've never stopped loving you, May. If my being there today is going to upset you . . . then I'd rather go home.

May Well, that makes me sound a real cow, doesn't it?

Terry No, of course it doesn't, I'll write to the kids, explain things, I expect you're right . . . I'd just louse things up if I stayed.

May Wow! I keep forgetting what a devious swine you are . . . for a second there I almost changed my mind . . . threatening to write and blame me, are you Terry? Well I'm calling your bluff . . . sling your hook then . . . piss off back to America. You could have saved the air fare. You should have sent her a greetings telegram, that's more your style.

There is the sound of a taxi's horn outside

Terry That's my cab.

They stand and look at each other

May (*brightly*) Well ... so long then ... till the next twenty years.

Terry picks up his bag and moves to the door where he turns and looks back at May

Terry I'm not quite the bastard you make me out to be, May. You weren't faultless you know.

May What did I do?

He puts down his bag and takes a step forward

Terry (*speaking with obvious sincerity*) When I fell in love with you, you were the prettiest girl I'd ever met—and the spunkiest—I was so proud of you ... You wanted kids—well, that was all right by me, I wanted us to have a family too—it's what life's all about, ain't it? But you changed, May ... I've taken a lot of stick about letting you down, well, you let me down. You changed from my girl ... into a mum.

May (*stunned*) Of course I did, I had kids to think about.

Terry (*softly*) But what about me, May? What happened to us? Where did the girl I married go? I had a girlfriend, I was proud to make her my wife ... then along came the kids and she vanished ... I had a mum, too tired to make love, not interested in going out ... having fun ... I felt like a wage packet in the end, my only asset was bringing home the money.

May That isn't true.

Terry It is true ... you know it's true, you even started calling me daddy when we were alone ... I wanted to shout at you: "The name's Terry, I'm not your bloody father!" Perhaps I should have ... what I'm saying is, we stopped talking to each other as people ... you pushed me to one side. I missed you, I wanted you back, not the perfect housewife and mother ... if I'd wanted that I'd have hired a housekeeper and a nanny ... you were so busy being an efficient housewife you forgot the word ends with wife ... Sylvie, she was just a symptom—not a disease.

May You're saying I lost interest in sex so you found someone else—the husband's standard excuse.

Terry (*shouting*) I'm not talking about sex, I'm talking about love—you know, love, the thing you women are supposed to have the monopoly on? I wanted you back, the girl I married, the one I fell in love with. (*Gently*) Where did she go, May? The girl I fell in love with.

May She was still there . . . she became a wife and a mother, it happens—it happens to us all.

Terry Not to us all. Some keep it, some get it right.

May (*softly*) Not too many . . . with most of us it gets swallowed up by real life.

The taxi horn sounds again

Terry I thought it would be different with Sylvie—a second chance. Trouble was I wasn't in love with her, not really . . . she loved me though . . . she gave it all to me.

May (*near to tears*) You mean she was easy sex when I was too tired from running around looking after your home and children.

Terry No, I mean she made me feel important, like it was us that counted—not just a wage earner, not just a provider . . . it wasn't her fault she wasn't you.

May (*defensively*) I thought you were important too. All right, maybe I did forget to show you, but for God's sake, Terry, you're supposed to be a man not a little boy. You should have told me you needed your ego boosting. I thought by looking after your home and kids I was showing I loved you.

Terry (*simply*) I'm just a bloke, May—not a saint. How often when I came home did you make me feel in the way? Just another mouth to feed. You never dressed up for me, made yourself pretty for me, showed me you still fancied me even. Maybe I am a selfish bastard but I wanted to . . . well . . . to feel important, as a person—not just a provider. I felt like I'd served my purpose for you, I'd fathered the children. When Sylvie came along, I suppose I was flattered: someone loving me, someone fancying me. You might think it's daft but I was feeling a bit unwanted.

May I loved you.

Terry Well you forgot to tell me, you didn't even really fancy me
any more—let's be honest. You didn't even talk to me other
than, "get the coal in, don't just sit around on your arse . . ." etc.
etc. You stopped talking to me—really talking I mean.

May (*desperately*) I didn't fancy anyone—I was too tired.

Terry (*simply*) Yes.

May Thousands of women do the same.

Terry Yes, and thousands of men wonder what happened to the
girl they married. Maybe they don't all bugger it up like I did,
but they miss their girls, May—they want their girls back . . .

The taxi hoots again impatiently

(*Moving to the door*) I'm not saying I was right, you understand,
I'm just saying it's how it all happened. The daft part is, I looked
for you in every other woman I met and I ran away from the real
thing—and why? Because we both failed each other—not just
me—both of us.

The taxi hoots again impatiently

Terry picks up his bag and walks away

May stands motionless as he goes through the door

May Terry!

He stops and looks at her

I thought you'd come all this way to see your daughter married.

Terry Not like this, May: not because I made you feel guilty—
thanks all the same. (*He turns go go*)

May How about because I want you too. How about because . . .
oh come on, for God's sake, they'll be sending out a search
party for me in a minute.

*May marches towards the door past Terry. He stands still and she
stops and looks back at him*

May And don't expect me to do the explaining, you're the one
with the gift of the gab.

Terry (*suddenly grinning at her*) You mean you're giving me a
second chance?

May (*walking off*) Don't get carried away, we're talking about the wedding that's all.

Terry Ah, but we're talking, May . . . we're talking!

CURTAIN

FURNITURE AND PROPERTY LIST

On stage: Sink
Cooker
Cupboards
Armchairs
Table
Coffee table
Ironing basket
Ironing board and iron
Clothes horse. *On it*: clothes including Bridal Veil, Bridesmaid's
    dress, Waist petticoat
Wooden windsor chair
Cordless phone

Off-stage: Airline bag **(Terry)**
Tray of drinks **(Dora)**
Cans of beer **(Dora)**

Personal: **Terry:** packet of cigarettes, handkerchief
Phil: watch

LIGHTING PLOT

To open: General interior lighting

Cue 1   **Terry:** "... she'll be over the moon."   (Page 3)
Cross-fade to spot L *on May*

Cue 2   **May** "... see you in church tomorrow."   (Page 3)
Cross-fade to the Goulds' kitchen R

Cue 3   **Dora** "... you'd better both start explaining your-   (Page 5)
selves
Cross-fade to spot L *on May*

Cue 4   **Dora** "... he had nowhere to stay."   (Page 8)
Cross-fade to the Goulds' Kitchen R

Cue 5   **Terry** "... I want us to talk."   (Page 19)
Black-out. Bring up spot L *on May*

Cue 6   **May** bursts into tears   (Page 19)

EFFECTS PLOT

MADE AND PRINTED IN GREAT BRITAIN BY
LATIMER TREND & COMPANY LTD PLYMOUTH

MADE IN ENGLAND